With

Water From The Rock

Poems flowing from a lifetime

Jean Clark

First published in 2007

Jean Clark
8 The Plantation
Christchurch Road
Norwich NR2 2BU
Norfolk,UK
jeanlclark@aol.com

Water from the Rock:
Poems flowing from a lifetime

ISBN 978-0-952871-36-X

Cover photograph Merigomish, Nova Scotia
taken by Jean Clark

Cover design by The Old Dog's Missus

Printed by Bell & Bain, Glasgow, UK

Contents

PREVIOUSLY PUBLISHED POEMS

'Caritas' from *New Christian Poetry,* ed. Alwyn Marriage. Collins/Flame (1990)

'Broken' from *Tapestry of Voices – Meditations on women's lives,* ed. Michele Guinness. Triangle/SPCK (1993)

'Broken', 'Still Centre' and 'Epiphany' from *Celebrating Woman,* ed. Janet Morley and Hannah Ward. SPCK (1994)

'Leaving You' from *Made for Each Other – Reflections on the opposite sex,* ed. Michele Guiness. Triangle/SPCK (1996)

THANKS

Thanks to Brian Thorne, and all those friends who give me support and encouragement – they will know who they are! And also my thanks to Maggie Taylor-Sanders for being the midwife to this book.

And when we meet
water breaks out of the rock
flowers bloom among stones.

Foreword

It is my privilege to have known Jean Clark as a friend and professional colleague for over half my lifetime. During that lengthy period she has never ceased to amaze me by her absolute fidelity to the voice within which is the guarantor of the integrity that permeates every aspect of her being. As she says in one of the poems in this astonishing collection, 'I take thee, spirit of truth to be my lodestar'.

Such steadfastness sometimes, of course, exacts a heavy price: it also demands emotional courage of the highest order. In her work as a therapist and in her personal relationships, Jean has been prepared to enter the unknown terrain of which the more faint-hearted can only have a dim awareness. She has also at rare times of extreme crisis shown a preparedness to move beyond the limits of consciousness and to risk herself in that treacherous land where the frontiers between sanity and madness are often lost in the mist.

For Jean the living of such a life has been made possible and at times incited by her gifts as a poet which seem to shine ever more brightly as she moves into her ninth decade. Her poetry is almost totally devoid of literary artifice. It is, rather, by turns a profound reflection on life's experiences and a challenge not to shirk the next stage of the journey. It is as if the poetry and the life are one as language is compelled to wrestle with the inexpressible and to illuminate mystery without depriving it of its transcendent and transforming power. The refusal to ignore the voice of the 'spirit of truth' means that Jean's poetry has a universal quality. As she grapples with the pain of failed relationship, the anguish of internal struggles, and questions of meaning and purpose, and celebrates the wonders of the natural world, the joy of new discoveries, the unexpected delights of old age, the amazing eruption of late-flowering passion, it is as if the whole kaleidoscope of the human soul's evolution is made available to us and we recognise not only the beauty of poet and poetry but also our own inherent glory. This is not merely the distillation of the joys and sorrows of a life lived to the full but a clarion call challenging us to take the risk of being fully human so that woundedness can be taken up into transfiguration. To read these poems offers the chance to discover anew the meaning of our own lives and the inspiration to embrace our destiny without counting the cost.

Brian Thorne,
Harlech, Holy Week 2007

Introduction: Poems flowing from a lifetime

I have written poetry for more than thirty years. A few have been published in anthologies of women's spirituality; some I have collected into booklets and given to friends and colleagues. I had not set out to be a poet; the poetry emerged when I was writing a journal as part of personal therapy and realised that prose was not adequate to describe my emotional world. Poetry had a rhythm, a flow which fitted the terrain of my inner journey. The poetry in this book tells the story of my life journey, and my spiritual journey. Poems like *Desert Journey*, *Beyond Chaos* and *It is Enough* show me the way.

During my fifties I wrote about the slow process of ending a long marriage, and then the move to a new way of life as woman alone, in my early sixties. One of these poems, *Broken*, found its way into two anthologies and I am told it has been used in healing services. During my seventies the poetry engaged with the questions, the emotions, the limitations and the insights of ageing. Then towards the end of that decade – but late – I found myself for almost two years in a passionate relationship, which was totally unexpected. Its poetry is in the final section of the book.

The poems continue to flow from a lifetime which has been and continues to be lived to the full. This is not 'literary poetry', it is poetry of the emotions, of the heart, of lived experience, and it seems that it speaks to people at stages on their life journey for which they cannot find words. When I was working as a therapist, owing much to Carl Rogers and the person-centred approach, I found that a poem could be a profoundly empathic response to my client's experiencing. Often they would discover that they too would find a new kind of clarity by writing poetry … a gift which they could carry into their lives after therapy ended.

I have recently had contact with a practitioner of Poetry Therapy and discovered that poetry is increasingly being offered to clients to help them identify their emotional state, and then perhaps write their own response. My approach has been to encourage the creativity which is in us all, by offering workshops on 'writing our feelings'. I have also worked in this way with groups suffering from mental health problems, eating disorders and the recurrence of breast cancer, and found that participants have often gained confidence and insight from the experience. A group of therapists has been meeting monthly at my home for over a year, where we write and then share our poetry; we value this space, which seems like no other, where we can quietly be with our thoughts and feelings and find metaphors for the journey.

We are living increasingly within a highly regulated society, with its targets and guidelines, and its stifling bureaucracy, and there seems little free space for creative energy to flow. My poetry is the only way I can express my frustration and my desire for space to play, to create, to collaborate, to become again community. I see straws in the wind … maybe the tight structures may loosen a little. I encourage you to write your feelings … to find your poet within.

Jean Clark, April 2007

Intimations

ORACLE

Cloud drifts
in quiet air
a pattern forms
flowering the sky.

Smoke rises
from the fire kindled
in the sacred hearth
at this ritual moment.

ROCKING RHYTHMS

While the train stands
at the platform
silence yawns,

when it moves
rocking rhythms cradle me
stilling mind and body.

Journeying gently
between destinations
suspended words softly
sound from deep places.
Why must trains stop
at unsuitable moments
in unnecessary places?
We need rocking rhythms
to hear the still voices.

WELLSPRING

Wellspring
water-head
thrusting up
through layers
of arduous rock.

Blood of the dragon
clarified, purified
bubbling joyfully,
welling with sadness,
reflecting light
downwards,
deflecting darkness
upwards.

A stone circle
keeps the spring,
its enclosure
giving power
and depth.

You may reach down
into the well.
There is always water
life depth
freely contained.

WHITE CAT

I met a white cat walking in the wood.
It was her wood, and she
the spirit who walks alone,
is very loving for a space,
then goes her way,
her coat gleaming in the morning
to see the things that cry out to be seen,
to hear sounds dropping from the sky.

And as we parted, she watched intently
something I could not see
or hear, but it was there
and as she moved, the wood grew.

STILL CENTRE

There is a still place where love is
and the way is very simple.
It is so simple
that I cannot understand
how hard it is to find the way
into the silence where love is.

LAND'S END

I dreamt I trod a causeway formed of rock,
the ocean to my left and the sea to my right.
Sea and ocean meet at the land's end.
I tread this rock-hard road
  moving westwards
    over peaks of a submerged
      mountain range
        salt waves lap my feet.

And in the distance
  within my vision
    the land's end,
      there where the sea
        and the ocean are one
          blue limitless.

I see only what I can see, feel what I feel
  because I am here now seeing the end
    where the last mountain
      falls sheer into the sea.

I am here in this place at this time
  laughing, running forward
    leaping onto steady rocks
      as waves wash
        over my sandaled feet.

Others are with me, behind my shoulder,
  I am not alone.
    They are the people of my journey,
      the necessary people
        who formed the pattern of my life.

Because they are there, I am here
    on this knife-edge-rock-road,
        this mountain range
            whose peaks create my way.

The ocean is very close,
    I can see where the road ends,
        and the sky is infinite
            in the near distance
                at my land's
                    end ...

JOURNEY TO SAINT ALBANS

I drive through fear,
cutting into the night
past monsters fleeing,
heavy in fumed blindness.

Headlong panic
driving past wrecks
of creatures dying –

    turn up words and music
    sounds of the world,
    blanketing fear,
    an incantation against terror.

It would be more fitting
to travel reverently
upon pilgrimage,
plodding on horses
through silent forests
where wild creatures lurk.
Moving slowly
sniffing the fear
scenting the danger.

Separations

TIDE WAY

Oh let us walk together over sands,
matching our footprints till they fill and fade.
Two salt-laced shadows whisper to the waves
and flicker by the edges of the strand.

Each moment drifts like weed beneath the waves
the ties that bound us move out on the tide.
The words we speak float past and leave no trace
upon the bleak wind blowing from the greying sky.

So let us take our ways where they will go.
My own path further yet beside that sea,
while you, impatient, wanting to be done,
turn back and drive to town along the road.

BATTERED ANGEL

We climbed the hill
to a small church stood
peacefully and stubbornly
for centuries
        (now men are quarrying
        the side of that hill
        to build motorways)
And inside, in the buzzing
late September silence
hovered with folded hidden wings
a very battered angel
        (they say she is
        the oldest angel
        still living in England)

She had sweet patience
in her eyes, regarding us,
she read the thought inside my heart,
the words soon to be spoken …
She saw the slowly burning fuse
lit long ago, the spark crawling
towards the explosive moment
that would destroy and then
reshape our world

My little battered angel watched me
as I wandered around the church
keeping my distance from the man
who once had been my life

Together, separating,
we came down from the hill

LEAVING YOU

'take what you must have and go'

I take what was mine
from what was ours,
dividing what cannot be shared,
deciding painfully how
to tear apart each thing
without breaking,
bleeding.

How can one home become two?
each single object halved,
a morsel for each.

So much between us,
eternity between us.
Deep rage between us
where once was love.

How can I halve my heart
that once was given to you?

BROKEN

Broken
by the wheel of the car
driving me to the next appointment.

Broken
by the tearing tensions
of demanding opposing
compartments of my life.

Broken
by the fall from the pedestal
on which I chose to stand.

Broken
by the disappointment
of those who thought me
strong and sure.

Broken
by angry taunts
of those who could not hear
my fear full words.

Broken
by words of bitterness and hatred
spewed from a dark
and unimagined place within.

Broken
by impermeable silence
unseen waves of mute resistance
and life denying loss.

Broken
the glass-like clarity of vision
into a thousand frosty fragments
splintering the ground.

Broken
steadfastly
as bread is broken
broken to be shared among us.

Broken
to be healed.

STILL UNBURIED DEAD

On my island life
shards of bone
lie unburied,
dust is heaped
against the sea side
of a wall, built
with stony silences.

Were there once corpses?
I never saw them,
no-one ever told me.
And yet I knew that wall
of raging, blocking pain
preventing loving,
joyful childhood playing.
  Silencing my songs
  Of angry innocence.

All those corpses
dust to dust,
never buried,
lying along the edges
of my life.

ABOUT PRISONS

In a prison, constricting
constraining walls
cut back humanity
to grey conformity
so that what may be experienced
is very limiting to the spirit.

Yet in some captives
that spirit
which will not be denied
breaks free in love

and the power of love
is greater than the prison,
the healing of love
more powerful than the wounding,
the bearing of wounds
more fruitful in the world
than hypocritical pretence
of virtue.

LIFE CHANGE

Change is boundaries dissolved
    space unlimited, reaching stars.

Change is being lost
    in strange unreadiness
    to end or to begin.

Change is fear
    of things unknown
    approaching.

Change is water flowing under bridges.
    A leaf carried by the flood
    to fortune – or to oblivion.

Change is mourning
    for things ended
    regret for things not done
    now never to be known.

Change is challenge
    to begin ever anew
    a letting go,
    renouncing,
    moving on
    to find an unpredicted
    life, now shaped.

EPIPHANY

at the end of a long marriage

'Today is my epiphany'
This is the turning point.
Change is coming,
the door stands wide
and there is no just cause
or impediment
why I should not walk through
into the liberation of the place beyond.

I choose
freedom
now.
I follow
my star
wherever
it may
lead.

I choose
dissolution
of false hope
dependency
security.

I take thee, spirit of truth
to be my lodestar,
in sickness and in health,
for richer and for poorer
forsaking all other.
I pledge my journey
to follow you
all the days of my life.

Resurgence

ISLAND GRAVE

Love died and was buried
in an island grave
beside the Venetian fort
on the last day of summer.

The grave dug
in rock hard, sun baked ground,
wreathed with rustling
gilded thistle heads.

Across the dancing blue
sea space, beckoned
a land – secret, dangerous.

There will be a journey
in spring,
to the unknown country.

NEED

a need – 'something necessary to life'

What was my need?
Being born – to be received
by gentle steadfast hands.
To be welcomed profoundly
by loving eyes meeting mine
bonding me in recognition
of who I am
and all I shall become.

What was my need?
To be fed generously
milk flowing, nurturing,
life giving, giving, giving …
And a voice saying
'Take, eat, all this is yours'.
Birth-rite, right to receive
love, freely given.
To be held in safety
Security of cradling arms.

What then was my need?

To grow in my own time.
The risks and adventures
of my becoming understood,
received and valued,
as I, growing, would be received and valued.
Not to feel afraid or guilty or ashamed
at my mistakes
upon the journey of my discovering.
Knowing I would be watched
with trust and love and joy.

What now do I need?
    Still to be recognised, confirmed,
    bonded by love.
    Held when I am afraid,
    accepted when I am angry,
    trusted when I push barriers
    of conformity out of my growing way.
    Deeply received, respected, loved.
    This is my need.

ROSES AND JASMINE

for Jane Ann

You gave me joyful welcome,
transformed my walls
to open trellis,
set roses and sweet
jasmine growing.

summer came again
when I had thought
winter had blighted
everything and always.

A rich and scented summer
bird-long and green growing,
buds swelling,
flowers opening, wide-eyed
in wonder.

Summer seeds fall
into autumn soil,
dive dying
into winter waiting,
rest till spring.

And now and always
spring comes to my heart,
flowering on my trellis,
jasmine in winter,
roses in summer.

MOVING ON

I have mislaid the pattern of my days
daily my house becomes less familiar
My story, now invisible, packed in cartons
symbols of my journey wrapped
in The Independent and The Sunday Times,
entombed in sturdy apple boxes.

Shelves grow empty,
corners of the room obscured
by bundled histories of my life.
Who am I now?

Daily the chaos grows without,
and yet within the dreams grow gentle,
saying to me 'yes, this is the path
you are to tread, carrying your tent,
removing, travelling, boundaries dissolved'.

This is the border land,
Where is your passport now?
What is the currency of your life
in this new place, unknowing and unknown?

I have mislaid the pattern of my life,
mislaid, and yet discovered peace.

STRAWBERRIES

Returning home,
I stopped to pick
strawberries.
Bent my head
bowed my back
ripened with them
in the sun.

THRESHOLD

For me
to write a poem
is passionate engagement
with that within
which calls persistently
for recognition.

It is my way
to reach below the threshold
of my conscious knowing
and discover
hidden words and images
releasing meaning
into life.

Travelling Woman

FLIGHT TO DETROIT

Eight hours to Detroit.
A scream of a flight,
'the Toddlers' Express'
frustration, howling,
screeching
a cacophony
of infantile rages.
No chance of exercise,
only their lungs
working overtime.

When I reach Detroit
and go through Security,
and Customs,
photographed
and finger-printed,
well …
I might just **scream!**

NIAGARA

Our boat moves steadily towards
that impossible
sheer fall
of water,
powerful, dangerous,
inexorable like death.

Going beyond terror, trust that we
could come so close
to utter destruction –
and live –
knowing the joyousness
of total surrender
to elemental forces.

In full awareness of our fragile strength,
and yet our glorious power
to feel, to know,
to laugh, to weep.

And the boat turns … and drifts again …
with the current … and we smile,
content that we shall always remember.

IN THE FALL

I am travelling
across the autumn of my days
on a train, in the fall,
and my spirit leaps into splendour.

So shall my fall be beautiful,
green growing golden
then flame like maple.

I always resisted autumn
but this is different,
so bold in beauty.
A celebration
before the season of bare branches,
when bones will bend
and frosts remind me
of mortality
and the icy ground.

Stay with me
through this fiery time,
warm your heart
in the flowering
of my fall.

WATERSHED

after crossing the Great Divide in the Rockies

When you cross the watershed
there is no way back,
if you are to flow with the river
you must go on.
There is no way back
to where you were
on the other side of the mountain.

You cannot even see
what once you saw
(only in memory),
you lived there once,
but now it is past.

Relinquish memory,
you have crossed the watershed.
Energy flows onwards
to another ocean.
There is no way back.

You may stop some time
and look into the distances
of yesterday's dying.
And there is no way back.

You will waste your spirit's energies
if you turn back
and try to struggle up the trail
to where you were, in youth
or middle age.
You cannot now go back.

Let go into what is now
    what is possible
    what is waiting
    what is calling.

It is winter, with all its variation
    of colour, space and light
    and deepening darkness.
    Tread boldly then
    through pine tall forests,
    greeting peaks and ancient ice fields.

There is no way back
to the other side
of the watershed.

BEAR AT SASKATCHEWAN CROSSING

a response to Mary Oliver's poem *Bear*

I saw it too, that naily footprint
scraped on the path, leading
to the lookout point!
on the edge of wilderness,
high above
the Saskatchewan River.

Should I be bold
and follow
to that space of risk?
        Or turn back,
        regain an illusion of safety,
        where only hidden creatures
        sting, and bring me low;
        never see the bear.

I did go on,
I took the risk,
said yes to danger,
real or imagined,
        and discovered
        in wilderness there is space
        to fear and rage and
        weep and love.

And yes, there was a bear,
I saw him the next day,
roaming along
the edges of the forest.

And there are bears
powerful and primitive
hidden in the forest
of my being –
and we may meet
if I continue on my way,
living dangerously.
bearing my life.

GRAND CANYON

I am enlarged within my spirit
by the immensity of creation.
The agony and the ecstasy
of history over millennia,
the oppression of women taken in battles,
the courage and the cruelty of trailblazers,
the poetry and the tenderness
of those who found their way into the depths,
swept by their passion,
through dark canyons by wild waters,
and in it all the depth,
the height, the width, the wonder
we may call the love of God.

CANADIAN FOREST WITH MAPLES

Patchwork
is too domestic a word
to describe
the hundred thousand colours
of a forest in Canada
in the fall.
You cannot adequately
describe the experience,
as you travel
hour after hour
through gleaming, burning colours,
sharpened with arrow tips
of dark green pines.

It is as if you sought
a single word
to describe a life
of deeply rich experiences,
layered with joy and pain,
laughter and tears,
loss and death,
gasps of wonder.
Adventures into hidden places
making discoveries
which suddenly gleam
with colours never to be repeated.

A life fully adventured
is a forest of a thousand colours,
and when the leaves fall
it is time to return to the earth.

RITA JOE

'poet laureate of the Mi'kmac nation'
Cape Breton Island, Nova Scotia.

Poet.
Elder.
Custodian of tribal wisdom
known and told through generations,
borne in hands scarred by living,
fully giving to her tribe.
Seeing, telling stories,
histories which must be told
and held and cherished,
and then passed on
to future generations
as gift.

Anchor woman to her tribe,
to all tribes –
wise words we need to hear.

MY STOMPING FIDDLING FRIEND

to celebrate 18 October 2004, when she bought a fiddle

Ann Marie
went shopping today
with a hey and a hoe
and a fiddle-dee-dee.

Made a dream come true
in a magical spree,
spent a hundred dollars
multiplied by three!
Up in Cape Breton
at the next ceilidh
you can watch her play
on her fiddle-dee-dee.

She will stomp as she fiddles
on her fiddle so free,
she's the happiest woman
in the whole countree.
With a dream come true
and her violin too,
she is ready to play
for the live-long day.
She's the happiest fiddler
in the whole countree
with a hey and a hoe
and a fiddle-diddle-dee.

VOYAGER

I have sailed
single-handed
through uncharted waters
over two decades,
learning, and leaning
into winds of change.
Contained, yet not constrained.
I travel where I will,
meet other voyagers,
am often alone.

Do I want
safe harbour,
to beach my boat
and go ashore,
to live
in uneventful peace?

Or shall I find a way
to travel in my heart and in my mind
to places yet unknown,
meet other fisher folk who travel
and return to tell their tales.
Smaller adventures, yet
enough to challenge spirit.

In the orchard

HAIKU

In the orchard
generous olive trees
offer grey-green shade.

A voluptuous orange
beckons,
'come to my scented tree'.

A sudden storm of sound
breaks through birdsong
quickening spring.

Four lemons
rest on the grass
remembering wild winds.

BEING AND DOING

All this doing
deletes the time
for being.
Doing for another
tangles the time
for being with.

The stream flows urgently
it is in its nature –
water nurtures growth,
washes despair out of chaos.
Till comes the time
to slow the flow,
reflect the sky,
receive a falling leaf,
floating it tenderly
to a space of calm.

Surely there are moments
in the day
simply to sit and be,
allow
uncover
discover
hidden knowing.

Is it too much to ask
my busy Self?

LEMON TREE

I am drawn to visit you
each time I walk in the orchard.
    You are not graceful –
    branches black and marked by time
    bark torn in places.
And is it winter fruit on those bare stems,
    while scent of spring
    meets me from tender tiny flowers.

One lemon fell when the great wind blew,
lies bruised, yet gleaming on the grass.
I pick her up, cup her in my hands,
breathe in the zest she holds
in ageing, pitted skin.

I meet my mystery
in the winter spring
of the lemon tree,
it mirrors cycles of my life
    where fruits and blossoms grow
    on branches marked by time.

ACEQUIA

The *acequia* is an ancient system of irrigation channels devised by the Moors in 12th century Spain. It carries the rainwater and the snowmelt from the high Sierra Nevada peaks to the valley farms.

Unexpected
unbidden
love comes
into the dry places
of my existence.
It pours
clear and fresh
from melting snows
on high peaks.
Flows
around my heart,
awakens hope
and trust.
Until my fears
are washed away
to fructify
the soil.

Love comes unbidden,
touching seeds
inviting growth,
opening buds
of laughter,
making tears flow,
refreshes spirit.
I give thanks.

LEAF

It is not about ending.
I cannot know how long
this leaf will hold
to the branch.

It has been
a late flowering,
then in due course
fruit ripened,
seeds grew strong,
scattered,
took root.

And the leaf
watches
rejoices
detaches,
then floats
falling to the ground
of her being.

It is not an ending.
It is completion.

I CAN ONLY PRAY

I can only pray
in places open to the sky,
enclosed in eternity.

I can only pray
to the silent God
who dwells in the mystery
of a flower opening,
a blade of grass growing
through concrete paths;
the complexity
of an ancient olive tree
whose roots go very deep.

My prayer is a breath of wind,
The love I feel in my heart,
snow in a high place.

I cannot pray
regularly to order,
on a particular day
in a particular way,
while my bones ache
on an unforgiving pew.
I cannot pray with those
who tell their god
what he should do.

I can only pray
in places open to the sky,
where my heart opens
to that mysterious God
who sings to me of love
and brings me truth,
and joy.

PROFOUND STILLNESS

Alone in the garden
not silent, for
birds sing in every tree,
but bone deep stillness
holds my spirit,
in moments
of profound
tranquillity.

Mountain weather

WILD CONTAINMENT

I am the wind blowing over the mountain,
I am the breeze in the orchard,
I am the sun on the high snows,
I am the bird singing in the olive tree.

Vivid energies
shaped by wind
sharpened by frost
coloured with nature's palette
of red and gold and green.

A wild containment
nurtures my vision,
frees my spirit
holds me fast
in space unbounded.
My soul sings.
Pure light
shines and fades.

I am the wind blowing over the mountain
I am the breeze in the orchard
I am the sun on the high snows
I am the bird singing in the olive tree.
I circle the earth
I circle you.
I am source and creation
I am …

STORM FORCE

At noon I sat alone,
quiet in the garden,
then
a breeze whispered
along the valley,
riffled the pages of my book,
cooled my burning skin.

I climbed the hill
through dancing flowers
a small wind supported me
as I walked
in peaceful meditation.

Supper with friends,
while outside
cloud drifted
over the valley,
obscured the moon's face.

Then bed, to sleep
after a peaceful sunlit day.
But no!
The wind blew
and the wind grew,
dancing a wild flamenco.
Storm force,
it battered trees
in endless hissing, tossing,
roaring rage.

I cannot sleep.

My sun-soaked body
turns and tosses,
the wailing frenzy
of maddened trees
assails my spirit.
And still I cannot sleep.

Morning breaks.
The sun emerges,
briefly,
to inspect the damage.

Then retreats.

WRITING THE WIND

I went outside to write a poem,
but
my pen fell into the swimming pool,
see it – there
shuddering with desire
to write.

Then the paper flew
kite-shaped
beyond my reach,
riding the wind
over the mountain.

Words spin
too fast to capture
too blurred to remember.
They are threaded, mismatched
along a string, creating
an incoherent necklace.

My creativity
        went shopping for clarity
                and has not yet returned …

WHAT THE WIND SAID

Terrible things have been happening
around the world.
It made me so angry.
I blew up.

I blew up your valley
roaring like lions
to frighten and distract you,
I knew I could scare *you,*
batter and confront you,
overwhelm you all,
like a tidal wave.

I had really intended
to blow all those warplanes
into the sea,
but it was just too difficult.
So I blew up your valley instead.
Sorry if I unsettled you.

IRAQ 2003

It is unreal, yet true
that we are heading into war.
I feel anger spreading
through my body …
What do they think will happen?
Blasting into action
both ill-advised and unaware
of implications for us all.

Across the years
I have written of my fear.
Fear that was personal –
        loss of a child
        a car crash
        estrangement from a lost love,
        death of friend,
        loss of my home,
        fear to live alone.
Fears devastating, yet human-sized.

Now the fear is manifest.
Missiles, destruction, bodies,
horrors displayed on television
endlessly fed into ears and eyes.
Sometimes I cannot bear to know.

Now the fear is global.
Terror lurks at the corner of the street,
in the railway station,
or a café frequented by the young.

Where will it end?
How can it end?
Have I rebuilt my life
only to fear destruction?

Now I am growing old,
I hoped to see my children's children
live in a world at peace
after years of wars.
A peace I hoped could be
born of will and trust.

But no, destruction
comes again.

A BITTER SWEETNESS

It has been a winter of deep frosts
biting the branches of the lemon tree,
shrivelling her fruits,
curbing the sweetness
of her flowering.

I weep for her limitations
as springtime comes again.
There is struggle,
as her shoots
make their weary journey
towards the sun.

When last we met,
she was battered
by wild winds;
her fruits, golden bright,
lay on the ground,
yet her perfumed flowering
lifted my spirit.

This year the fruits are brown,
still cling to branches
afraid to fall.
Is it her time to rest –
then fruit again?
Or is it time,
having lived fruitfully,
to die?

Remembering

JENNI
14th March 1957

Candles burn
remembering
griefs unheard,
unwept,
put aside
to create a kind
of normality,
buried in a common grave
as if of no consequence.

Still the pain stings,
the shame of bleeding,
waiting to lose
the child I had not wanted.

My child and I
were separated,
in cold, clinical, hurried
ways. Never seen,
never held, no tears allowed.
Only now I realise
that we were both
abandoned.

Without Jenni,
our family
did not come to fruition.

Her hidden, unspoken death
marked a beginning,
a long slow awakening
to an intensity of losses
never grieved.

Today I recognise,
it was the beginning
of the ending of
a marriage.

LEAVING HOME

It was a bitterly
primitive
experience,
imprinting scars upon psyche,
so that, though
two decades have passed,
still the pain echoes
year upon year.
Remembering rejection
of all that had been
honourable and good.

Still the sharp memory
of a last day
in a spacious home,
the hours before leaving,
a night, fearful
yet truthful.

Opening the door
to a life of uncertainty,
walking out
for the last time,
the most agonising
liberating steps
of a life, till then
secure.

EMERGENCE

It was an impasse,
no way to go but through
and out into winter darkness,
frost and mist and snow.

There was an angel,
yes truly she was there,
invisible, taking my hand
guiding me to each place
of sanctuary,
day by day.

It was more than survival,
it was emergence
from the chrysalis
built layer by layer,
year by year,
to protect my spirit.

The air was damp and cold,
but the sense of wings
opening, spreading,
was deep and true.
It was far more than survival,
it was life flowing
through my veins,
free at last to be,
to sing, to fly.

JE NE REGRETTE

I celebrate
my choices,
my not choices,
my saying 'no'
and my saying 'yes'.

I celebrate
the paths I have taken.
I do not wish
even to consider
what might have been.
Everything has had its place
in my life's journey.

Yes, there came a time
of recognition,
that I had become
constrained
from following my truth,
my path of intuitive knowing.
I chose another road
as yet unknown,
and journeyed on.

I do not have a list
of 'might have been',
I make my choice each day
and live with what will come.
Je ne regrette rien.

Another mile or ten

DESERT JOURNEY

Richard Holloway writes of God's absence as 'a place of committed unknowing'.

I hold deeply
to what I cannot
know. I trust
profoundly
the mystery
of my existence,
the miracle
of my loving
and being loved.

I belong
with those
who are dispossessed
of certainty.
I am alone
in the singing
silence.
A fertile void
uncluttered
by dogma.

IT IS ENOUGH

It was a long and hidden journey
travelling from Him to Her
then to the Mystery
which now invites my spirit.

Not knowing
where I was going
or why I was compelled.
No group of companions
no map, no signs,
only the knowing
it was the time
to challenge security,
to endure unknowing,
to risk undoing
the certainty I had assumed
till now.

Now I have gone
beyond gender
beyond naming
and taming.
I only know
the ground
of my becoming.

All I can accept
is the Mystery.
It is enough
to die for.

HOW LONG?

How long do I have?
'As long as you are' she said.

I am
So long as my heart is open
my eyes see and wonder
my ears hear the silences,
my words flow into poetry.
So long as I love.

And when I have danced my life,
then let me go
into a place of stillness,
rapt in silence
life completed
lived.

MY NEST

This tree stands tall
branches spread wide,
roots reach down,
touching lurking fears
and griefs hidden,
experienced, full felt,
and now become
rich soil filtering
into cracked and splitting
rocks of denial,
creating security.

I have been there,
discovered the holding strength
of the taproot of that tree
on the cliff edge,
and I have flown
to the topmost branch
seeking freedom.

One branch reaches out
beyond security
to the edges of the wind.
I have pitched my nest
on the tip of this branch.

It is where I must be.

WHO PAYS?

I shall simplify my life
for it has become
very complicated,
filled with regulation,
notification and forms
filled with information.

Cultivating a society
of blame and claim
and counterclaim,
deadening trust.

To work is risk,
however careful
however skilful,
life happens.
Shall we remain
in boxes, never open
to the storms of living?
Shall we stifle creative energies,
cover and smother
        till they break free
        in frustration
        and destruction?

Then we can blame,
then we can claim.
But who pays?
Why me?

WHY NOW?

Sometimes
a jagged lump of rock
is flung into my river,
splintering the surface,
stirring muddy waters,
blurring clarity.
Sometimes
timber falls from the bank,
blocks the flow of thought,
obstructing creativity.

Until within my heart
and mind,
the woman and the man,
each skilled in ordering
their own known
spheres of action,
come to the river, and
gently, methodically
put all to rights.

Till then I must rest.
Prepare to remember
the pattern which enables
a semblance of security.

The channel clears,
water flows.

MI JUBILACION

Time packaged
in hour-shaped
boxes, filled
weekdays,
Monday to
Friday.

Weekends –
shopping,
washing,
cooking,
packaging,
freezing,
cleaning.

Now
time flows
into interesting shapes,
along
uncharted pathways.
Sometimes pauses …
for snoozes …
Then wakes, laughing,
with space for fun!

SLOW

Slow
is about evoking
a new kind of clarity,
a time to look
and see
what we had not
noticed previously.

The very word
slows the breath
inviting sounds
which were not there
before.

TAKING TIME

This morning
I took time by the hand,
and together we washed
and dressed,
very slowly.

Sun streaming
into the bathroom;
enjoying the softness
of water showering my back.
Choosing clothes
suitable for a cold bright day.

Doing a little necessary
kitchen work,
slowly,
thoroughly.

Then sitting,
seeing
the blue sky,
framing
great and beautiful trees,
all waiting
for me to slow my pace,
to live each moment.

At last, after eight strange months
I am discovering
what it means
to stop
work.

BEYOND CHAOS

It comes nearer,
the next ending,
leading initially
though chaos –
that necessary seedbed
for what may come.
I do not need structure
or planning, only
the letting go.

Wait,
be still
hold the silence
within your heart
and maybe something
new and unexpected
will emerge and grow.
The creative thought
which is hidden
beyond chaos.

ANOTHER MILE OR TEN

Autumn into winter.
Shall I choose to pretend
eternal spring?
Or relinquish slowly
my pride of energies,
        accept your hand
        helping me up the hill.
Receive gracefully
        your willingness
        to serve sometimes
        my need.

Independence is
seductive,
necessary,
laudable
        and yet can become
        stubbornness
        overweening pride,
        boring self-sufficiency.

I look back
and there have been
sharp bends in the road,
rivers to swim,
quicksands to negotiate.
I often chose the stony path,
scaled peaks with wide vistas,
crossed watersheds.

Shall I choose now a kinder way?
my river flowing gently
till she merges with the sea.

LATE HARVEST

Gradually
inhabiting
a space reshaped,
cleared of clutter.
Last year's nest
made ready for rebirth
and a new phase
of existence.

A tangled vine
now pruned
severely,
invites new shoots
fresh and green,
prepared to fruit again.
Later there will be
A mellow vintage.

And then, but late

THE WAVE

I had thought my tides
of energy were retreating
in my ageing. Sands
drying, strands
of water crossing
a stony beach.
Time for quiet
certainties, calm seas
reflecting pale blue sky.

Then suddenly
comes a wave of energy
breaking, overwhelming
my cave of rock,
challenging my quiet life.
New energies awaken
bring emotions
unconfined
by propriety.

WILD CARD

You disconcert me.
Always before, I knew
how to keep control
of situations,
stand in a safe place,
knowing what to expect,
what to do, and how to feel.
When love was measured
into orderly spaces,
where I kept myself
secure. I had
no expectation
that a force of caring love
would overturn
my settled existence.
Then you came
into my sufficiently
satisfactory life.

You disconcert me,
come from unexpected directions
at irregular times, unsettle
planning, which would,
keep me safe from risking
an uncertainty of loving,
acceptance of no commitment,
this nest on the tip of a branch
which may blow one day
into the sea below.

One comfort is that
I think that you too
are disconcerted!

FIRE SEED

Long years
the fire seed lay dormant;
ponderous clay
dampened her spark,
weighed upon her heart.

She glowed sometimes
gave light to others, but
no flames
flowered in her.

Until the moment, when
she wept her pain,
at loss of what was not
and never now could be.

Her cry was heard.
The casing of the seed
melted in a wondrous
glow of love,
given and received.

Passion unleashed,
the fire seed
flowed into a trembling
place of trust,
flowered into flames,
then slowly grew
into peaceful loving.

SAFE HARBOUR

Choosing to sit
in a café at the water's edge
beside the harbour,
waves lapping gently
soothe my senses as I wait.
Flowers bloom
in tubs on the pavement,
spilling colour into my life.
Time passes – hours and minutes –
will the ship come soon?

My eyes are blurred
sometimes with tears.
He may be facing storms,
cross-currents I cannot know
or see. And yet a sense
deep within the waters of my sea
knows, and thrills with expectation.

He slips into harbour,
sails a little tangled,
struggles of the voyage
showing in his eyes.
Safe for a few short hours
we meet in gentle waves,
of tender celebration.

We had to wait
for the tide …

GIFT

Thirsty ground
receives rain
thankfully,
without protest
or resistance.

Roots of plants
drink gladly
and grow
their acceptance
of gift.

Perhaps we,
who feel compelled to give,
can learn how to receive
from others,
without guilt or reluctance.
Finding fulfilment
as we grow
peacefully
into the pleasure
of becoming
fruitful.

MY HAND IN YOUR POCKET

Yesterday
we walked on a deserted beach
hand in hand like two children,
daring the tide line,
dark waves driving towards us
propelled by cold
east winds.

Hold the moment,
it will not happen again
in that place.

Hold the experience,
my hand in your pocket
holding yours, sharing warmth
and comfort.

The wind brings tears,
isolation carries
fragile freedom.

Yesterday
it happened,
and the memory
warms our hearts.

RISKING EVERYTHING

Truly to live, deeply to love
brings in its wake
risk.

Not just the word,
but the reality
of fear, pain,
unexpected disapproval,
even rejection.

When we risk,
a window opens
to unexpected,
joy and tears,
cowslips carpeting
a meadow,
water softening ground
once dry and barren,
fire in the heart's hearth.

Risking everything
is the challenge
to live with eyes open,
knowing reality
knowing fragility
not demanding
certainty.

Risk is revelation
of being,
moment by moment,
alive.

GIFTED WITH SUNSETS

You have gifted me
with a joyous
sense of my being
more fully woman.
Brought me alive
in ways never dreamed,
challenged me
to reveal
more of who I am
in darker hidden places.
Pulled my hands from my eyes
so that I can no longer hide
in confusion and incoherence.

You have gifted me
with sunsets,
held me
in undemanding ways,
yet demanded
truthful exchange …

LOVE IN BEING

for Adam Curle

Being in love
is a madness
a burning heat
of passion,
challenging, exciting
sometimes demanding.

Love in Being
is of a different order.
It grows out of stillness,
compassion and giving
of self to the grief
and the pain and the rage
in the world.

Truly to Be
is a lifetime's journey.
Truly to love
is the heart of the matter.
It will change you
for ever.

TEA FOR TWO

I prefer tea
which is poured equally
into two mugs.
He and I sitting
side by side
listening to each other
drinking in
each other's needs
to be known and valued.
And when we separate
we go our ways refreshed.

FREE ENERGY

'regulate – *the flow of the river has been regulated*'

A river's flow
may be
regulated
controlled
adjusted
managed,
dammed
with good intentions.

Yet
its powerful energy
can break free
and overwhelm
people and homesteads.
When our energies,
for political
rational reasons,
are blocked
side tracked
and monitored …
ignoring the need
to explore and experience,
they become
potentially destructive
even
dangerous.

Creative energies
released
nurtured,
valued, and
free to flow …
may bring inspiration
new perceptions
new life.

Coda

YEAR'S END

Two leaves,
swinging, clinging,
twisting, tangling,
dancing, wrestling.
A courageous reluctance
to separate, let go
float to earth
reach oblivion.

Wild wet winds
invisible adversaries
testing tenacity,
will you be there
in the morning?

I wake
only one leaf
clings and swings
awaiting
the year's end.

Tomorrow
the branch
will be bare.

ECLIPSE

A full bright moon,
the sky clear,
or so it appeared,
no storm clouds
on the horizon …

As we spoke our truth,
a dark shadow
began to creep
across the face
of the moon,
slowly obliterating
her glowing face.

All seemed lost,
no light to see
a way forward.

Heart stopping darkness
like death.
Time passed,
no rain fell,
only tears.

At midnight
we looked up,
saw beads of light
along the rim
of the still darkened moon.
A gleam of hope,
that may shed light
upon a world

profoundly changed
during that time
when darkness.
divided us.

REMEMBERING FRIDAY

All night it seemed
held in tenderness,
waking to passion
and the pain of letting go –
        such loss.

But the weather was gentle,
early spring blossomed
along the road
we had not travelled
before.

A map of the new journey
towards a separation
from your arms
holding me.

One more day together,
knowing reality
and yet so tender,
holding each other close,
passion not far away.

Strange how this decision
has brought us
closer,
to care so deeply,
within a place
which has no words.

LIMINAL SPACE

A time of transition
from lover to friend –
how could it be other than disturbing,
  confusing,
  draining,
  enlivening?
I feel energies
tingling in my body
not yet knowing
how or where to go

A confusion.
  A cornucopia
  of loss and hope,
  fear and challenge,
  uncertainty and strength,
  trust and the desire
  for this new way
  of being together apart.

I am intensely aware
of a price to be paid
for our willingness
to be so deeply shaken,
to the very core it seems.
          Not to cut off
          shut down
          let die
something so valuable
as our connection,
born of profound knowing
each of the other.

A SILENT CHORD

I can find no word
for the strength of our connection
through many times of crisis
over so many years.
It is beyond caring,
deeper than affection.
It is a thread woven
from strands of truth,
intuition,
and trust.

RELINQUISHMENT

Reality begins to bite
as the world holds a mirror
to our ageing,
our limitations
of energy,
of memory.
'Diminishment'
the word tolls.

Shall we listen,
shall we hear the messages?
'Let go, let others, let be.'

Relinquishment is
a space of dignity,
where dreams may blossom
and spirit shines.

CARITAS

She has lived
you can see it in her face,
loving that left her with
marks of a thousand sorrows.

She has lived
in ways the world judges
unsuitable
unlovely
unacceptable.

She has lived
life to overflowing,
in valiant risk-filled
encounters with freedom.

She has loved;
broken painful caring
for others in that world,
(people in need are often
unbeautiful, unloved).

She has loved
you can see it in her eyes,
gazing in certainty
of pain and joy and wonder
at the world's being.

And the lines of her loving
and the clarity of her vision
and the effort of her living
hurt in her healing heart.
She has lived.

CRONE

Crowned, white haired,
face lined with loving,
knowing the pains of growing.
Well deep wisdom.
  Tribe mother,
  godmother,
  wise other.

She sits so still in the sacred space,
in the centre, and on the edge
of mystery, moving towards dying.
Offering the newborn arms
comforted by lifetimes of holding,
grieving, hurting, loving, crying, dying.
Hands knowing fullness and emptiness.

    And where is she now and here?
    Sitting staring, arms empty,
    hands knotted with impotent energy
    often debased into troublesome child.

I would be Crone,
wearing the white ash crown,
respected and honoured by the tribe,
  for my being
    my living
    my knowing
    my remembering
    my forgetting.

I will sit in the sun
in the place of my choosing
in the space of my waiting,
until I am ready
in my own time
and in my own way
to say 'goodnight'.

And my name will be remembered.
Tribe mother
Godmother
Wise woman
Crone

Index